My first book of
Animal babies

by Miranda Smith

Natural history consultant:
Dr. Kim Dennis-Bryan
F.Z.S

Tick
Tock

An Hachette UK Company
www.hachette.co.uk
Copyright © Octopus Publishing Group Ltd 2013
First published in Great Britain in 2013 by TickTock, an imprint of
Octopus Publishing Group Ltd, Endeavour House, 189 Shaftesbury Avenue, London WC2H 8JY.
www.octopusbooks.co.uk

ISBN 978 1 84898 257 4

Printed and bound in China
10 9 8 7 6 5 4 3 2 1

Cover photography: front, main, Steve Bloom Images/Alamy; background, Bob Gibbons/FLPA;
back, above left & right, Creatas Images/Thinkstock; centre & below left, iStockphoto/Thinkstock;
below centre, Flip Nicklin/Minden Pictures/FLPA; below right, Hemera/Thinkstock

contents

Words that appear in **bold** are explained in the glossary.

Meet the animal babies

Nearly all the animals on Earth begin their lives as babies. In this book, you can explore all the different kinds of baby animals that there are in the world.

Most animals in the world are **invertebrates**. This means that they do not have a backbone or an internal skeleton made of bone. The rest are **vertebrates**, or animals that have backbones.

Most animals, including invertebrates, are **cold-blooded** – their body temperature is controlled by their surroundings. Birds and mammals are **warm-blooded** and can maintain their own body temperature.

Fish

Fish are cold-blooded vertebrates. Most of them lay eggs, but some give birth to live young. The fish babies in this book include the great white shark and the salmon.

Insects

Insects are invertebrates that usually hatch out of eggs as larvae or nymphs. Most of them do not get any care from their parents before or after hatching. The insect babies in this book include the dragonfly and the weaver ant.

Mammals

Mammals are warm-blooded vertebrates. Most mammal babies are born live, usually from their mother's body, and feed on their mother's milk. The mammal babies in this book include the American black bear and the blue whale.

Birds

Birds are warm-blooded vertebrates that hatch out of eggs. The babies are called hatchlings. The bird babies in this book include the albatross, the cuckoo, the ostrich and the penguin.

Arachnids

Arachnids are cold-blooded invertebrates with eight legs. Most arachnids lay eggs, but some scorpions give birth to live young. The arachnid babies in this book include the garden spider and the scorpion.

Reptiles

Reptiles are cold-blooded vertebrates. Many reptiles hatch out of eggs, but some are born live from their mother's body. The reptile babies in this book include the Nile crocodile, the green mamba and the Komodo dragon.

Amphibians

Amphibians are cold-blooded vertebrates. Most of them start life in water. They usually hatch out of eggs as larvae and breathe using gills. The amphibian babies in this book include the common frog, the fire salamander and the midwife toad.

A world of animal babies

The map on this page shows our world.

There are different land masses on Earth. They are called continents. Asia, Antarctica and North America are continents. The blue areas on this map show the different oceans of the planet. The Indian and Pacific are two of these oceans.

Animal babies are found nearly everywhere in the world. Some of them are found in only a few places, while others are found on many different continents. Some of them are born in water. Some are found in rivers and lakes and others in the very deepest oceans.

When you read about an animal baby in this book, see if you can find the place where they live on the map.

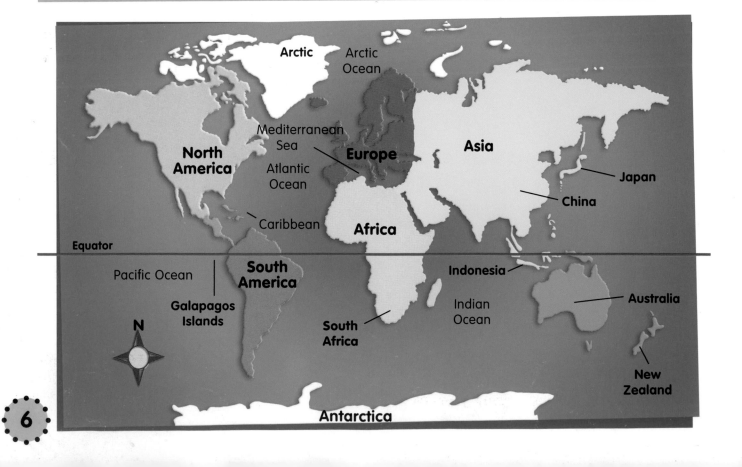

Animal baby diets

Some animal babies, like tiger cubs and seal pups, only eat meat or fish. Other animal babies, like baby elephants, only eat plants. Many animal babies, such as bears, like to eat meat and plants!

Look for these pictures in your book. They will tell you what kind of food each animal eats.

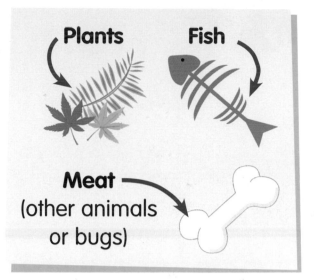

Plants   **Fish**

Meat
(other animals or bugs)

Animal baby habitats

Some baby animals live in hot places. Others live in cold places. The different types of places where animals live are called **habitats**.

Look for these pictures in your book, and they will tell you what kind of habitat each animal lives in.

Deserts: hot, dry, sandy places where it hardly ever rains

Polar lands: cold, frozen places at the very top and bottom of the earth

Mountains: high, rocky places

Lakes, ponds, rivers or streams

Oceans: a saltwater habitat that covers most of the Earth

Deciduous forests: forests with trees that lose their leaves in winter

Coniferous forests: cold forests with trees that stay green all year

Rainforests: warm forests with lots of rain

Grasslands: dry places covered with grass

American black bear

American black bear cubs are born blind, nearly hairless and helpless. Their mother nurses her two or three babies in her warm **den** during her winter **hibernation**. She feeds them on her milk.

The mother bear shows her cubs how to find berries, insects, nuts and seeds to eat.

Fantastic fact!

Bears break open beehives with their paws and lap up honey with their tongues.

Where are American black bears found?

The bears live in North America, from Alaska and Canada to northern Mexico.

In spring the baby bears come out to explore. They clamber up trees if there is any sign of danger.

Elephant

As soon as an elephant calf is born, its mother helps it to stand so that it can start to feed. The calf cannot see well but recognizes her by her smell, the sounds she makes and her touch.

By the time it is eight months old, the calf has learned to use its trunk to eat and drink. It will continue to feed from its mother for up to ten years.

Fantastic fact!

Elephant calves are more hairy than adults. Asian calves have the most hair of all.

Where are elephants found?

The biggest elephants live in Africa. Smaller ones live in Asia.

Elephants have a long childhood. They live in a group where all the **herd** members look after and help to teach the young.

Blue whale

A baby whale, or calf, is born tail-first. Its mother helps it towards the ocean surface where it takes its first breath.

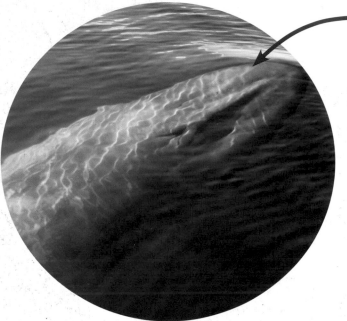

The blue whale is the largest mammal on Earth. Every day it eats 5 tonnes of **krill**, tiny shrimp-like creatures that it filters from sea water.

Fantastic fact!

A fully-grown blue whale can grow up to 30 metres long. Its heart is about the size of a small car.

Where are blue whales found?

Whales are found worldwide in the sea.

The new baby weighs about 2.5 tonnes and is 7 metres long. It stays with its mother for eight months.

Chimpanzee

A mother chimpanzee carries her baby as she travels through the rainforest with her **troop**. At night she builds a nest to sleep in, often sharing it with the baby's older brothers and sisters.

By six months the chimp is able to hold onto his mother's fur, so he can ride on her back. She shows it how to find food such as fruit, seeds and plants, and dig out termites with sticks.

Fantastic fact!

Like people, chimpanzees smile. They hug other chimps and hold hands.

Where are chimpanzees found?
Chimpanzees live in western and central Africa.

A mother chimp may have several young of different ages. The older brothers or sisters often help to carry the younger ones and play with them.

Harp Seal

Once a year mother harp seals gather to give birth to pups on the Arctic ice. They feed their pups on milk for about 12 days then swim away.

The pups keep their white coats for about two weeks. After that, dark hair grows under their white fur and turns them grey.

Fantastic fact!

Seals can remain underwater for up to 30 minutes.

Where are harp seals found?

The seals live in the North Atlantic and Arctic oceans.

The newborn pup is covered in white fur to hide it from polar bears and hunters. It will be two more weeks before it can swim or find fish to eat, so it is in great danger.

Echidna

A female echidna, or spiny anteater, digs a **burrow** and lays a soft-shelled egg. She keeps the egg warm in her pouch. It hatches after ten days. The baby is called a puggle. It is tiny, blind and hairless.

For up to six months the puggle feeds on milk released through **pores** in its mother's skin. Then it catches ants and termites with its sticky tongue.

Fantastic fact!

Echidnas are **monotremes**, the only mammals that lay eggs.

Where are echidnas found?
Echidnas live in Australia and New Guinea.

After about seven weeks
the puggle leaves the pouch.

It begins to grow
spines for protection
and hair for warmth.

Grey-headed flying fox

The female flying fox, or fruit bat, gives birth to a pup once a year. For the first three weeks she carries it with her everywhere, even on her night-time hunts for fruit, **pollen** and **nectar**.

When the pup gets too heavy, it is left behind in a 'camp' of thousands of flying foxes that hang from the branches in forests or **mangroves**.

Fantastic fact!

Flying foxes live until they are about 15 years old.

Where are grey-headed flying foxes found?
The flying fox lives in eastern Australia.

Young flying foxes are able to fly by the time they are about three months old. This fruit bat is one of the largest bats in the world. Its wingspan when fully grown measures more than a metre.

Hippopotamus

A mother hippopotamus gives birth away from the **pod**, usually underwater. When the calf is born, she helps it to reach the surface to breathe.

The fierce mother protects her calf from crocodiles, lions and hyenas. The calf often rests on her back and stays close to her when she sleeps.

Fantastic fact!

Female hippos are called cows. They stay together in groups called **schools**.

Where are hippos found?
The hippopotamus lives in Africa.

The calf can feed from its mother underwater, closing its ears and nostrils to stop water getting in.

Harvest mouse

Harvest mice live in hedgerows and among tall grasses in the fields. A female harvest mouse can give birth to up to three **litters** of babies in a year. She has 1–7 young, called pups, at a time.

This harvest mouse baby is 17 days old. It is sharing a grasshopper with its mother, close to the nest.

Fantastic fact!

Like a monkey, the harvest mouse uses its tail to keep its balance while climbing.

Where are harvest mice found?

Harvest mice live in Europe and Asia.

A female harvest mouse builds a round nest of woven grass high above the ground. When her babies are born, they feed on her milk for two weeks, then venture out to find fruits, bulbs and insects to eat.

Lion

Lions live in **prides** of around 15 animals. There are two or three adult males – the rest are females and cubs. The lionesses give birth to a litter of 1-4 cubs.

The adult males in a pride vary in their behaviour towards cubs. Some let the cubs play with their tail or mane. Others snarl and may even bat the cubs away.

Fantastic fact!

Lion cubs are born with spots on their bodies that fade as they grow.

Where are lions found?

Lions live in Africa and northwestern India.

Newborn cubs are tiny, helpless and blind. They open their eyes after about a week, and can walk after about three weeks.

For seven months the cubs **suckle** milk from any of the female lions in the pride.

Bottlenose dolphin

A bottlenose dolphin calf is born underwater, usually tail-first. It is immediately helped to the surface by its mother to breathe air. Sometimes other females from the pod help as well.

Dolphins can dive for more than 5 minutes, but they spend most of their time near the surface. They are fast swimmers, and often leap out of the water.

Fantastic fact!

Dolphins navigate and hunt for food by making high-pitched sounds that bounce off objects.

Where are dolphins found?
Bottlenose dolphins live in oceans worldwide.

28

The mother feeds the calf on her rich milk for 18-20 months. Then it learns to hunt for fish and squid with the pod of up to 15 dolphins.

Bottlenose dolphins are friendly and intelligent animals. They communicate by a range of clicks, squeaks and whistles. The calf can recognize its mother's sounds.

Bactrian camel

Bactrian camels have two humps. These store the fat that they need to survive in the desert. The females usually give birth to one calf at a time, and it feeds on her rich milk for up to 18 months.

In winter, the young camel has a long, shaggy coat to protect it from the freezing conditions. In spring, the coat peels off, leaving it with very little hair.

Fantastic fact!

Camels' eyes are protected from the wind and sand by a double layer of long lashes.

Where are Bactrian camels found?
Central Asia, Mongolia and China.

A newborn Bactrian can stand within a few minutes and walk just a few hours later. It has very small humps.

Over the next five years the calf grows until it weighs more than 600 kilograms and is 2 metres tall.

Red deer

Red deer males are called stags, and the females are called hinds. The stags often fight each other with their **antlers** to win females. After mating, the hinds often gather in large herds.

A baby deer is called a fawn. At first, it is left hidden alone while its mother is feeding. Its spotted coat helps to **camouflage** it in the grass.

Fantastic fact!

Hinds bark when frightened and moo when calling to their young.

Where are red deer found?
Western red deer live in Europe and northern Asia.

32

A fawn can walk almost as soon as it is born. It feeds on its mother's milk for two months.

Zebra

A zebra family group has one male stallion and up to six female mares and their foals. A mare gives birth to a single foal and feeds it for a year.

Foals are brown and white but adult zebra are black and white. Their striped coats confuse **predators**, such as lions, that cannot see their shape properly when they run.

Fantastic fact!

Zebra are often found in mixed herds with wildebeests and giraffes.

Where are zebras found?
Zebras live in eastern and southern Africa.

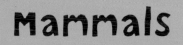

Each pattern of stripes is unique, which means that zebras can recognize each other.

Polar bear

A newborn polar bear weighs just 0.5 kilograms and can fit into its mother's front paw. Most of them have twins. The cubs are born in winter inside an **ice den** where the mother is hibernating.

The milk of a polar bear is very rich, and the cubs grow quickly. The female and her cubs come out of their den in spring to find food.

Fantastic fact!

Mother bears spend all summer eating and storing up fat so that they can feed their cubs through winter.

Where are polar bears found?
Polar bears live in the Arctic.

The female polar bear is fiercely protective of her cubs. She needs to look after them. As well as the danger from wolves, they may be attacked by adult male polar bears.

Wolf

A she wolf gives birth to a litter of five or six cubs in a den among rocks or underground. The cubs are blind and deaf at birth and stay in the den with their mother until they are **weaned**.

Young wolves grow up as part of a **pack** in which there is a strict order. The younger wolves have to give way to older animals at feeding time.

Fantastic fact!

Each wolf pack has an **alpha** male and female and they are usually the only ones to breed.

Where are wolves found?
Wolves live in eastern Europe, Asia and parts of North America.

The older wolves protect cubs at nursery sites and hunt for food while the cubs play and sleep.

Young cubs often have darker fur.

Red fox

The female red fox, or vixen, gives birth to litters of about five cubs in an underground den. The male dog fox brings her food. The newborn cubs are grey and do not open their eyes for two weeks.

Fox cubs play together. They also fight each other to establish which is the strongest, and which one gets food first.

Fantastic fact!

The fox uses its thick tail to help it to balance, as a warm wrap in winter and a flag to signal to other foxes.

Where are red foxes found?
Red foxes live in North America, Europe, Asia and Australia.

At about five weeks old, the cubs start to explore outside. They still feed on their mother's milk for up to ten weeks. Then they begin to hunt for small **prey** such as mice.

Koala

Koalas are **marsupials** that live in trees. A female koala gives birth to a blind, hairless, earless joey. The joey crawls up into a pouch – an upside-down pocket on her stomach.

The joey feeds on its mother's milk, growing ears and fur. At six months it leaves the pouch and rides on its mother's back.

Fantastic fact!

The koala's pouch is closed by a special muscle that the mother can adjust.

Where are koalas found?

Koalas live in Australia.

Koalas live on a diet of eucalyptus leaves. As the joey grows it eats its mother's **pap**. These are special droppings that help the joey to digest the tough leaves.

Kangaroo

Kangaroos are marsupials. A newborn kangaroo, or joey, is only 2 centimetres long and hairless. There may be different joeys of different ages in their mother's pouch at one time.

This joey is 30 days old. It has made the journey to its mother's pouch and attached itself to one of her four teats. It feeds until it is several weeks old.

Fantastic fact!

Red kangaroos can hop at up to 34 miles an hour and jump up to 8 metres in one bound.

Where are kangaroos found?
Kangaroos live in Australia, Tasmania and New Guinea.

As the joey grows, the muscles in the pouch tighten. This is so that, when its mother hops, the joey does not fall out. The growing joey spends time outside the pouch, feeding on plants, until it leaves the pouch at about ten months old.

Nile crocodile

Nile crocodiles nest on sandy shores or riverbanks. The female digs a hole and lays about 50 eggs. She buries the eggs in sand, then guards them carefully for three months.

Hatchlings are about 20–30 centimetres long and the parents lead them or carry them to water in their mouths.

Fantastic fact!

Female Nile crocodiles nest close together and look after each other's hatchlings.

Where are crocodiles found? Nile crocodiles live in Africa.

The hatchlings make high-pitched chirps inside the eggs when they are ready to hatch. This is the signal for the mother crocodile to uncover the nest.

The mother rolls the eggs in her mouth to help the shells open.

Eastern green mamba

Male green mambas often compete to mate with a female. These **venomous** snakes dance and wrestle with each other. The female lays 5–17 eggs, usually in a nest in a hollow tree.

Green mambas spend most of their lives in the trees, only visiting the ground to find prey such as frogs, lizards and small mammals, or to bask in the sun.

Where are green mambas found?

Eastern green mambas live in east Africa.

The young mambas hatch out about three months after the eggs have been laid.

They use an **egg tooth** on the end of their nose to make a hole in the egg. They are about 40 centimetres long and bluish in colour. They change to a bright emerald green as they grow.

Komodo dragon

A female Komodo dragon lays about 20 eggs in a burrow in the side of a hill. The young dragons break out of the shell with an egg tooth that then drops off. They dig themselves out of the burrow.

Komodo dragons have long, **forked tongues** that they use to detect food. Young Komodos eat insects, eggs, geckos and small mammals.

Fantastic fact!

Komodo dragons can detect **carrion** from about 5 miles away.

Where are Komodo dragons found? Komodo dragons live in Indonesia.

Young Komodo dragons are very vulnerable at first. They spend much of their early life in trees to avoid predators. The dangers include adult Komodo dragons that are **cannibals**.

Green turtle

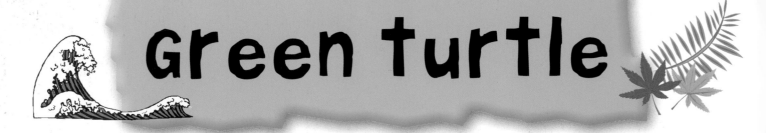

Green turtles spend all their lives in the sea but lay their eggs on land. Every two to four years female green turtles return to the beach where they hatched to lay their own eggs.

The female turtle hauls herself up the beach, far away from the water. She digs a hole in the sand and lays about 130 eggs. She then covers the eggs with sand and returns to the sea.

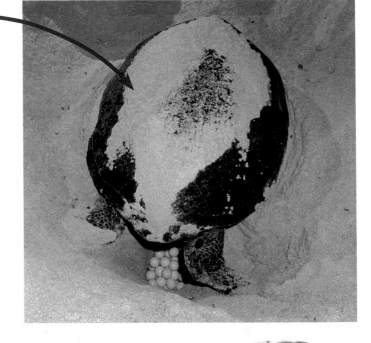

Fantastic fact!

Green turtle hatchlings are less than 5 centimetres long and weigh less than 25 grams.

Where are green turtles found?

Green turtles live in the Atlantic, Pacific and Indian Oceans.

When the eggs hatch up to three months later, the babies dig their way out and make a dash for the water, as seagulls swoop in to snatch them up. The survivors reach the sea, but face dangers from predators there as well.

Honey bee

A queen bee spends all her time in the nest and lays hundreds of eggs every day. These are fertilized by male **drones**, and hatch as **larvae**. They become **pupae** before emerging as adults.

The bees' nest is usually in a hollow tree. There they build sheets of six-sided wax cells that form a honeycomb.

Fantastic fact!

The larvae that become queens are fed all the time on a special substance called **royal jelly**.

Where are honey bees found?

Honey bees are found all over the world except the Arctic and Antarctic.

Some of the cells of the honeycomb contain eggs or the hatched out larvae. Others are used to store the honey, which is used as a winter food.

Dragonfly

Dragonflies mate in flight and the female lays her eggs on the leaves of underwater plants. The eggs hatch into wingless creatures known as **nymphs**. The nymphs live underwater, feeding on plants.

When the nymph **metamorphoses** into an adult, its skin splits. A dragonfly with wings crawls out and flies away.

Fantastic fact!

Dragonflies are among the world's oldest living creatures. They were flying 300 million years ago, before dinosaurs walked the Earth.

Where are dragonflies found?
On all continents except Antarctica.

Most of a dragonfly's life is spent as a nymph. It lives in ponds or slow-flowing rivers, eating insect prey.

As nymphs grow they get too big for their skin. They cast it off and emerge larger, growing more like an adult each time.

Garden spider

Garden spiders mate in autumn and the female makes a silken **egg sac** for the eggs that she lays. She hangs the sac on her web and stands guard.

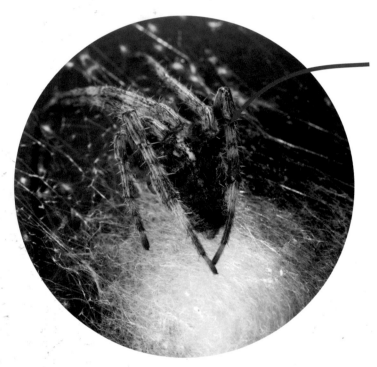

Each spider produces up to four sacs, each containing hundreds of eggs. While she is looking after them, she does not hunt for food. She dies before they hatch out.

Fantastic fact!

The female garden spider sometimes eats the male after they have mated.

Where are garden spiders found?
Garden spiders live in Europe, Asia and North America.

In spring, tiny yellow spiderlings emerge. They spin a mass of silk and cluster in a ball until they **moult**. Then they leave by 'ballooning' – using a thread of silk to hitch a ride on a puff of wind.

Ladybird

There are several stages in a ladybird's life. A ladybird lays eggs that hatch into larvae. These pass through four growth stages before changing into pupae.

The ladybirds hatch from the pupae. They are pale-coloured at first, but get darker and spots appear.

Fantastic fact!

The larval stage lasts three weeks. In this time each larva eats several hundred **aphids**.

Where are ladybirds found?

All over the world except the Arctic and Antarctic.

Ladybird larvae hatch and feed on **aphids** and other prey. They shed their skins as they grow bigger.

After feeding, they attach themselves to plants and form a dome-shaped pre-pupa. This hardens and becomes the pupa.

Weaver ant

Colonies of weaver ants are begun by a female known as a queen. She lays her **clutch** of eggs on a leaf. She and worker ants protect and feed the larvae when they hatch out.

Weaver ants make their homes from living leaves. They do this with help from their larvae, which produce a sticky white silk thread.

Fantastic fact!

When weaver ants bite, they also spray poisonous formic acid into the wound.

Where are weaver ants found?

Weaver ants live in Africa, Asia and Australia.

Worker ants begin to build the leaf nests by pulling leaves together.

They then pick up larvae in their jaws and use their silk thread like glue to bind the leaves into a ball.

Monarch butterfly

The monarch butterfly is famous for its migration south to spend winter in the warm. On the way north the following spring, the females lay eggs. Emerging butterflies join the journey northwards.

Each larva spins a green chrysalis. Inside, it is transformed, emerging after ten days as a beautiful winged insect.

Fantastic fact!

Each new generation of monarch butterflies returns to the same group of trees.

Where are monarch butterflies found?

Monarch butterflies live in the Americas, Europe, southeast Asia and Australia.

The wormlike larvae are called caterpillars. These first eat their egg cases, then feed on the milkweed plants on which the eggs were laid.

Scorpion

Scorpions give birth to live young. Each young scorpion is white and surrounded by a thin skin-like membrane. They free themselves from this, and one by one, climb onto their mother's back.

When male and female scorpions are ready to mate, he grasps her **pincers** and they do a mating dance.

Fantastic fact!

Scorpions have curved tails that end with a venomous stinger. They use it for defence and to make large prey helpless.

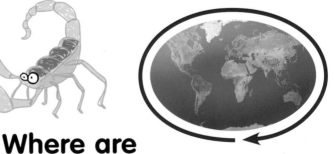

Where are scorpions found?
Scorpions live in hot climates around the world.

Young scorpions stay on their mother's back for several weeks. When they have moulted at least once, the young climb down and scatter in search of food.

Barn owl

Female barn owls lay their eggs in holes in trees or in old buildings such as barns. They lay up to seven eggs over two or three days. When hatched, the young are different ages and sizes.

The owlets eat more than their own body weight each day. Both parents hunt for mice and other small mammals, frogs and insects.

Fantastic fact!

Barn owls often swallow their prey whole and cough up pellets of the bits they cannot digest.

Where are barn owls found?
Worldwide except in desert and polar regions.

When the owlets hatch they are covered in white **down**. After about 60 days they have adult **plumage**.

Emperor penguin

The female penguin lays one egg on ice in late autumn, then swims out to sea to feed. For nine weeks the male keeps the egg warm, balanced on his feet, covered with a flap of feathered skin.

Male emperors huddle together in the icy wind, taking turns to move into the cosiest place in the middle.

Fantastic fact!

Penguins cannot fly but they can dive deeper than any other bird, and stay under water for 20 minutes.

Where are emperor penguins found? Emperor penguins live in Antarctica.

When the fluffy chick hatches, it is covered in a layer of down. When the female returns, she **regurgitates** food for it. After this, the parents take it in turns to fish for food.

ostrich

These flightless birds are the largest in the world. They also lay the largest eggs – 20 centimetres long. The male ostriches take charge of the babies, though males and females share in raising young.

After four weeks, the young can run fast enough to keep up with an adult. Male ostriches may look after several families together. The chicks follow them wherever they go.

Fantastic fact!

Ostriches can run at up to 40 miles an hour, and use their small wings for balance as they run.

Where are ostriches found?
Ostriches live in Africa.

Ostrich chicks hatch about 40 days after the eggs are laid.

Their brown feathers help to camouflage them against the sandy soil, often saving them from predators such as hyenas and jackals.

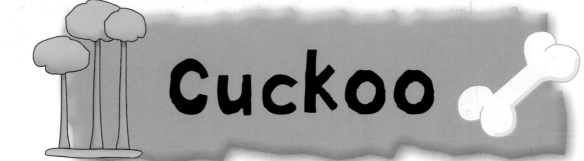

Cuckoo

Many cuckoos lay their eggs in other birds' nests. The female leaves one egg in each nest she visits. Often these nests belong to much smaller birds.

The cuckoo chick is often the first to hatch. It pushes any other eggs out of the nest.

Fantastic fact!

The cuckoo's favourite food is hairy caterpillar. It bites off the head and shakes out poisons the caterpillar absorbs from plants.

Where is the common cuckoo found?

The common cuckoo spends spring and summer in Europe, then returns to Africa or Asia.

The foster parents, such as this male Cape Batis, feed the baby cuckoo with all the food they can collect. They believe it to be their own, even when it is much bigger.

Golden eagle

Golden eagles mate for life. They build large, untidy nests called **eyries** in tall trees or on high crags. They often use the nest for several years, adding to it each year.

The female usually lays two eggs that both parents take turns to **incubate**. The chicks hatch out after about 40 days.

Fantastic fact!

Golden eagles dive on prey at up to 150 miles an hour.

Where are golden eagles found?
Europe, Asia, North America.

The chicks are covered in fluffy white down. They are looked after for seven weeks until they are big enough to make their first flight. Sadly, the youngest chicks often die, because they can't compete with the older chicks for all the food.

Albatross

Albatrosses build nests in high places, such as cliffs, near the sea. The female lays a single egg, and the parents take turns to incubate it.

Albatrosses leave the nest to find food, which they store in the upper stomach. When they get back to the nest, they regurgitate the food for the chicks.

Fantastic fact!

Albatrosses spend most of their life airborne at sea and even sleep while they are flying.

Where are albatrosses found?
The Southern Ocean, the south Atlantic and Pacific oceans.

Both parents continue to care for the chick for several months. They feed it squid and fish until it is ready to fly. The chick will launch itself from the cliff-top.

Mute Swan

Swans usually mate for life. They build a large nest a metre across on the ground near water. The female lays up to nine eggs and the pair take it in turns to incubate the eggs for about 40 days.

Baby swans are called cygnets. They ride around on their mother's back for safety. The male often hisses and beats its large wings to protect its young.

Fantastic fact!

Male and female swans look alike, but the male is usually larger.

Where are swans found?

Mute swans live in Europe, Asia, North America, Australia and New Zealand.

Mute swan families stay together while the cygnets grow. The young swans have short necks when they hatch and are grey-brown in colour.

Their necks get longer as they grow and it takes nearly a year for their feathers to turn white.

Fire salamander

Fire salamanders mate on land. Then the female places her eggs, in batches, into shallow streams, sometimes over a period of several months. The eggs hatch as larvae as they touch the water.

The larvae develop into black and yellow adults that live on land. They feed on small prey such as spiders, grasshoppers, flies, beetles and worms.

Fantastic fact!

They are called fire salamanders because, when people made fires of the logs in which they hid, they would emerge, as if born of the flames.

Where are fire salamanders found?

Fire salamanders live in Europe and northwest Africa.

There are usually between 20 and 70 larvae. Each has four legs and is about 2.5 centimetres long.

The larvae breathe with feathery gills, and feed on minute insects in the water for about three months.

common frog

The female common frog lays up to 4,000 eggs at a time in water. They are fertilized by her mate as she releases them, coated in a jellylike substance for protection. This **frogspawn** floats in the water.

The eggs hatch into legless tadpoles with tails that gradually develop legs. Later, the tadpoles absorb the tail, becoming froglets.

Fantastic fact!

The common frog breathes through its skin. It hibernates on land in piles of rotting leaves or mud.

Where is the common frog found?
Common frogs live in Europe.

Tadpoles metamorphose into froglets over a period of about 14 weeks. Tadpoles have gills that allow them to breathe underwater. Froglets have lungs and gulp in air to breathe on land.

Midwife toad

These shy, **nocturnal** toads mate on land. The female produces a string of eggs that the male fertilizes. He wraps the string round his back legs to keep them safe until they hatch as tadpoles.

The tadpoles grow quickly and metamorphose into toadlets, growing legs and crawling onto land. By day they hide under stones, coming out at night to feed on insects.

Fantastic fact!

The small **warts** on the back of the midwife toad give off a smelly poison when the toad is attacked.

Where are midwife toads found?

Midwife toads live in western Europe and northern Africa.

The male midwife toad may carry several strings from several different females. Just before they are ready to hatch, he lowers his legs into shallow water, and the tadpoles emerge.

Great white shark

The eggs of the great white shark hatch inside the female. The pups grow inside her until she gives birth. There are up to ten pups in a litter and they measure around a metre in length.

By the time the pups grow up, they have up to 300 triangular teeth. These are in rows that move into position as the old ones wear out.

Fantastic fact!

Great whites can detect one drop of blood in water up to 3 miles away.

Where are great white sharks found?

Great white sharks live in oceans worldwide.

The minute a great white pup is born, it has to swim quickly away from its mother. If it does not, she may think it is prey and eat it.

An adult will grow to around 5 metres long.

Salmon

Salmon swim upriver to **spawn**. The female lays her eggs in a **redd**, which she digs in gravel with her tail. When the male has fertilized the eggs, she covers them with gravel.

Adult salmon travel enormous distances to reach the river where they were born. They leap up waterfalls and over obstacles on their way upstream to spawn.

Fantastic fact!

Salmon fry feed on yolk sacs for four weeks before they dig their way out of the gravel.

Where are salmon found?

Salmon live in the Atlantic and Pacific oceans.

When the eggs hatch, the young salmon, called fry, wriggle out through the gravel to find food.

Seahorse

Male and female seahorses swim side by side, change colour and 'dance' for several days before they mate. She then lays the eggs in a **brood pouch** on the front of the male.

There are usually 100–200 eggs in a litter. The male seahorse carries the eggs until they hatch out. The young then swim out through a hole at the top of the pouch.

Fantastic fact!

Seahorses are one of the few species on Earth where the males carry unborn young.

Where are seahorses found?
Seahorses live in warm oceans worldwide.

After up to 25 days the eggs hatch, the father expels the fry and the female lays another batch in his pouch.

Only about one in 200 of the young survive to adulthood.

Glossary

alpha The alpha male and alpha female are the leaders in a wolf pack.

antler Bony growth on the head of a deer.

aphid A tiny insect that sucks sap from plants.

brood pouch A kind of pocket made of skin on the front of a seahorse.

burrow A hole or tunnel in the ground made by an animal to live in or escape from predators.

camouflage A pattern or mixture of colours that helps an animal to blend into its surroundings.

cannibal An animal that eats its own kind.

carrion The flesh of a dead animal.

clutch The number of eggs produced or incubated at one time.

colonies Groups of animals that live together.

den The shelter of a wild animal.

down The soft, first feathers of many young birds.

drone A male bee. Unlike the worker bees, drones do not collect honey or pollen.

egg sac A case made of silk that contains the eggs of a female spider.

egg tooth A growth on the tip of a beak that a bird or reptile uses to break out of its egg when it hatches.

eyrie The nest of an eagle, built high up, on a mountainside.

forked tongue A tongue that splits into two parts at the tip.

frogspawn Fertilized frogs' eggs surrounded by a protective jelly.

herd A group of grazing animals comprising a male, females and young.

hibernation Spending winter in a sleeping or inactive state to survive the cold.

ice den A dug-out cave in the ice that a polar bear makes to spend the winter in.

incubate Sit on eggs to keep them warm.

krill Tiny, shrimp-like ocean creatures.

larva (plural: larvae) A stage in the life of an animal between hatching and becoming an adult.

litter The number of young born to an animal at one time.

mangroves Forests that grow on tropical coasts.

marsupial A type of mammal. Most carry their newborn babies in a pouch.

metamorphose To change in body shape as an animal grows.

monotreme A type of mammal that lays eggs. Echidnas and duck-billed platypuses are monotremes.

moult To shed an outer covering, such as skin or feathers.

nectar A sugary fluid that plants make in their flowers.

nocturnal Describes an animal that is active after dark.

nymph A young insect that is a tiny copy of its parent without wings.

pack A group of animals, such as wolves.

pap Semi-liquid food.

pincers The claws of a scorpion.

plumage All the feathers of a bird.

pod A small herd of dolphins, seals, whales or hippos.

pollen Tiny yellow grains, or dust, found in flowers, that helps to make seeds.

pores Tiny openings in the skin that allow sweating.

predator An animal that hunts and eats other animals.

prey An animal that is hunted and eaten by another animal.

pride A family group of lions.

pupa (plural: pupae) Stage in the life-cycle of an insect, during which its adult body is formed.

redd The dug-out nest in gravel where a salmon lays its eggs.

regurgitates Brings up food; some birds and mammals do this to feed their young.

royal jelly A substance produced by worker honey bees. Fed to larvae for three days and to queen bees.

school A group of fish, dolphins, whales or female hippos.

spawn The mass of eggs laid by some animals, including fish and amphibians.

suckle To drink milk from an animal.

troop An animal group.

venomous Describes an animal that is able to produce venom.

wart A rough lump growing on the skin.

weaned Describes when a young animal begins to eat adult food.

Index

Picture credits

Alamy Alison Thompson 63; Barry Bland 20; blickwinkel/Artwork 87, Hecker 66; DanieleC 21; Dave Marsden 51; David Gowans 77; David Wall 50; Design Pics Inc/Keith Levit 8; Fabio Pili 73; FLPA 55; Frank Blackburn 76; Ian Hainsworth 33; Papilio/Jamie Craggs 93; WildPictures 86
Ardea Bob Gibbons 59
Corbis Minden Pictures/Piotr Naskrecki 62
FLPA Biosphoto/J L Klein & M L Hubert 24, 25; Dave Pressland 85; Derek Middleton 84; Frans Lanting 53; Imagebroker 9, Imagebroker/Christian Hütter 61, Hans Lang 68; Jürgen & Christine Sohns 69; Minden Pictures/Colin Monteath, Hedgehog House 31, Flip Nicklin 13, 29, Ingo Arndt 67, Konrad Wothe 15, Michio Hoshino 16, Mike Parry 89, Mitsuaki Iwago 44, 52, Rene Krekels/FN 57, Richard Du Toit 35, Tui De Roy 70, 71, 79, ZSSD 23
Getty Images Art Wolfe 72; Darren Moston 80; Dr Clive Bromhall 92; Gerry Ellis 41; Hiroya Minakuchi 91; John Cancalosi 81; Minden Pictures/Konrad Wothe 39
iStockphoto.com Kativ 58
NHPA Anthony Bannister 49; Daniel Heuclin 83; Dave Watts 19; Martin Harvey 46
Thinkstock Altrendo Nature 40; Comstock Images 37; Design Pics 38; Digital Vision 74, Anup Shah 27; Hemera 12, 60, 65; Ingram Publishing 90; iStockphoto 2, 3, 10, 11, 14, 18, 22, 26, 28, 30, 32, 34, 36, 42, 43, 45, 48, 54, 56, 64, 78, 82, 88; Photodisc/Anup Shah 51; Stockbyte 75, Tom Brakefield 1, 17